ᓄᓇᒥ ᐆᒪᔪᑦ ᐱᐊᕋᖏᓪᓗ

NUNAMI UUMAJUT PIARANGILLU

ADULT AND BABY ANIMALS ON THE LAND

ᑎᑎᖅᑐᒐᖅᑐᖅ

ᐃᒪ ᐲᑕᓴᓐ

TITIQTUGAQTUQ ILLUSTRATED BY

Emma Pedersen

ᐅᓇ ᓇᓄᖅ.

Una nanuq.

This is a polar bear.

ᐅᓇ ᐊᑎᖅᑕᖅ.

Una atiqtaq.

This is a polar bear cub.

ᐅᓇ ᑐᒃᑐ.

Una tuktu.

This is a caribou.

ᐅᓇ ᓄᕐᕋᖅ.

Una nurraq.

This is a caribou calf.

ᐅᓇ ᐊᒪᕈᖅ.

Una amaruq.

This is a wolf.

ᐅᓇ ᐊᒪᕈᐊᕋᖅ.

Una amaruaraq.

This is a wolf pup.